Love, From Grandma

Words of wisdom and hope from America's grandmothers

Becky L. Amble

Future Focus Publishing
Minneapolis, Minnesota

Published by Future Focus Publishing
A Division of Future Focus
2626 East 82nd Street
Minneapolis, Minnesota 55425-1381
(612) 858-8877

Copyright © 1994 by Becky L. Amble and Future Focus

All rights reserved. No part of this work may be reproduced or
transmitted in any form or by any means without express
written consent of the publisher.

Photo illustrations used with permission of Dave and Louise Olsen
of Dave Olsen Photography, Inc.

Copyright © 1994 by Dave and Louise Olsen and
Dave Olsen Photography, Inc. All rights reserved.
513 South Washington Avenue
Minneapolis, Minnesota 55415
(612) 332-1084

ISBN 0 - 9643203 - 0 - 4

Printed in the United States of America

For information on Future Focus publications or services
call (612) 858-8877.

Dedication

To Grandma Betsey

Acknowledgements

All the Grandmothers

Louise & Dave Olsen, Dave Olsen Photography, photo illustrators

Tabor Harlow, Harlow Associates, Inc., book design

Carol Ratelle Leach, editor

Jo Haugen, editor

Kimberly Kroubetz, editorial assistant

Unlimited Partners by Elizabeth & Robert Dole, published by Simon and Schuster

Norman Vincent Peale, Ph.D. and Sybil Light of the Peale Center for Christian Living

A special thank you to Tessie for her diligent help, and to Dave and Louise for the photo illustrations and hours of encouragement.

Thank you to all of the people who passed out my questionnaires, and especially to all of the women who took the time to write their advice. I wish we could have used everyone's material.

All of the Grandmothers have given me permission to use their first name, initial of their last name, age, and either home town or current residence.

About the Author

Becky L. Amble

Becky L. Amble is an accomplished businesswoman, marketer, and researcher. She has been cited as a trendspotter by *The Wall Street Journal* and *USA Today*. She owns and operates Future Focus, a company that helps businesses develop growth strategies. She is also involved with several professional, civic, and community groups.

Becky grew up in North Dakota and now lives with her husband, Marshall Gravdahl, and two cats, Alexandra and Greta, in Woodbury, Minnesota.

Introduction

I started this book nearly three years ago. The idea came about as a result of my business and workplace trend research. I noted several trends indicating a high level of stress, frustration, and uncertainty among Americans of every age. I thought a book of advice from Grandmothers who are caring, sincere, and experienced would provide some comfort.

This book has really had a life of its own. After I sent out a short questionnaire, things started to happen. The questionnaires started coming back from women throughout America. I read the responses the day I got them. I was struck by the love in the advice and with the appreciation the Grandmothers expressed to me for writing this book and including them in it. I finally realized that God and the Grandmas were in charge of this book.

I believe God made Grandmothers different from everyone else. They are special, yet more than that. They love us unconditionally just as God does. They hold us close to their hearts and protect us. They are like beacons of light, millions of them—there to guide us and show us the way, if we just look and listen. They can be there for us forever, if we let them.

My own Grandma Betsey was a special person in my life—the only living grandparent I ever knew. She was in her early 70s when I was born, yet she never seemed as old as her years. A courageous and strong woman, she lived her last thirty years in darkness. You see, she was blind. Her life couldn't have been easy. Grandma grew up and lived on a farm in North Dakota. She lived in a nice, well-built home when I was young, but I know it wasn't always that way. She was born in 1881 and I know it was a different world then. Grandma lost two children who didn't live beyond the first few years of their life, and lived thirty years after Grandpa died. Even though she survived many tough times she was always calm, serene, and kind.

We went to visit Grandma Betsey often, and she also came and stayed with us. She lived alone in her house most of the time. Grandma kept her house up and cooked for herself, which I always thought was amazing since she was blind.

My best memories are of sitting with Grandma. She would rub my back or we would sit and hold hands or play her hand game (where you alternate putting hands on top of each other's). She even taught me a little Norwegian. We didn't have to do anything special. It was special just to be together.

Grandma Betsey continues to be a guide to me; a gift from God. She has helped me with this book and continues to "be there for me". If your Grandmother is still living, I hope you will make the time to be with her and enjoy her. If she is no longer with this world, she can still be with you in spirit and in memories.

Love, From Grandma is more than a book of advice; it is a book of love. As you read through the pages I hope you will explore and experience this love and share it. All of these women wrote their advice because they love their grandchildren. Maybe your Grandmother is in the book or maybe she is speaking through one of these Grandmothers.

Becky L. Amble

Foreword

Our grandmothers often define the very best in us. Childhood memories of lessons learned at her knee become lessons to be followed in adulthood. The grandmother's position is an enviable one; all the good parts of listening and loving, playing and reading, praising and spoiling without the daily routine and problem solving. Her role allows nurturing and coaxing. From the vaulted position of a grandmother she can speak volumes about what's good and right and honest and pure. A grandmother can instill values and morals and truth through her wisdom and warmth.

Even today, when families are scattered, torn apart by the forces of our age, a grandmother can perform a service to youth. Even over a distance a grandmother can communicate by mail, by fax, by phone; kind of an electronic knee. It misses some of the touch, the smell, the feel, but the influence for good growth is still present.

My grandmother, Laura Peale, lived with her banker husband Samuel in the little rural Ohio town of Lynchburg, some 50 miles from Cincinnati. My brother Bob and I were dispatched by our parents to spend the summer vacation time in those healthful and supervised surroundings.

I remember the smell of the house and the freshness of the green grass surrounding it. Here I learned to love the vanilla ice cream which was served at church socials. Bedtime in the darkened upstairs bedroom Bob and I shared meant nighttime prayers; stern words urging good behavior mingled with praise for Jesus and all He does for little boys.

Bob and I were not that good and I know at times we disappointed Laura and Samuel. We'd learn straight away of their disapproval and perhaps feel the strap or hear a vigorous reprimand. All the while, though, we knew we were loved. Somehow we also knew we were learning great life lessons. In later years Bob and I often spoke of those summers and of our devoted grandmother.

One memory stands out. We, of course, attended church every Sunday in the company of our grandmother. It was a small Methodist church of the style of the time. The sanctuary was rather square-shaped and the pews formed a semicircle, one behind the other facing the pulpit and choir loft. Dressed in our scratchy Sunday best we'd follow our grandmother into the church and to the familiar seats we always occupied. Laura Peale would separate the young brothers, one on either side of her, so as to forestall any troubling disturbance during the lengthy service. We squirmed and fretted. Before long my grandmother's soothing hand would rest on my knee as if to say, "It's only a little longer, Norman. Be still and listen to the great words of the Bible and hear those unforgettable hymns. This is important, Norman. You are learning about the goodness of God."

That soft and gentle hand of my grandmother was always gloved during church. And to this day I can smell the rich leather aroma of the black kid Sunday gloves, and I remember her, I remember all she taught me and I give thanks for the eternal truths I learned from my grandmother.

– *NORMAN VINCENT PEALE, Ph.D.*
Rawling, New York
August, 1993

Love, From Grandma

Take care of yourself.
Love,
Grandma

Your future lies in your hands. Earn respect for who you are and what you stand for. Be strong about your beliefs and what you want to accomplish in life. Most of all, remember that you are a complete person and cannot look to others for happiness. To be happy and loved, love and be happy. Stay young in heart and share life with those who earn your love and respect. Don't look for happiness; happiness is inside you.

—*Jane W., 58, Minneapolis, Minnesota*

The most important person is you. Look at yourself in the mirror. Is this person your friend? You may fool the world down the pathway of years and get pats on your back as you pass, but your final reward will be heartache and tears if you have cheated the person in the glass. Think for and be yourself.

—*Elaine R., 68, Naples, Maine*

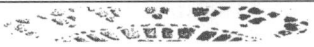

Life is short and hard work, so make it count for something. Remember that no matter what you do, it always affects someone else. Be ready not only to accept the congratulations but also the responsibility. Use your mistakes to learn.

—*Jeanette S., 56, Monterey, California*

Accept yourself and value your uniqueness in the world. Be curious and continue to learn new things as long as you are able. Surround yourself with loving friends and family, and be in touch with your spiritual being. Love yourself so you can love others.

—*Nell S., 57, Newman Grove, Nebraska*

Always be honest with yourself first; it will extend automatically to others. Honesty keeps you in control and able to deal with all of life's situations.

—*Muriel O., 67, Thompson, North Dakota*

Always remember that you are unique; there is no one else like you. You are a child of a loving God and have inherent and infinite worth. Understanding that enables you to fulfill your unique potential, a condition for abundant living.

Take one day at a time. Be forgiving, understanding and kind, and to thine own self be true. Strive for harmony in relationships, and enjoy the "journey."

—*Christina S., 75, Spokane, Washington*

Nowadays, many are trying to influence you, usually for their own gain. It is vitally important that you think for yourself and hold steadfast to your beliefs.

—*Elizabeth L., 78, St. Paul, Minnesota*

Be responsible for all you say and do.

—*Mary D., 53, Peoria, Illinois*

Love, From Grandma

Be true to yourself always. Think highly of yourself and don't let the negative from others wear you down. Love other people as brothers and sisters. Be kind, courteous, and supportive. Meditate frequently on the Word of God, and look to Him for strength and guidance.

—*Roxann M., 54, Mounds View, Minnesota*

Be a leader and not a follower. Stay away from drugs, including liquor. Be kind to everyone.

—*Dorothy I., 84, Superior, Wisconsin*

Be up front with your feelings; don't sacrifice your feelings if you are being hurt for someone else's pleasure.

Learn to laugh at your minor mistakes and learn from the ones that shook the earth. Have a sense of humor and always be a good friend to the people who are good friends to you.

—*Sharon K., 49, Chicago, Illinois*

Don't postpone joy in the beauty of life's rhythms. Let no television program lure you from enjoying a sunset.

FIND YOUR GREATEST CONTENTMENT IN YOUR OWN COMPANY.

Don't postpone the great adventure of READING biographies, history, short stories, and essays. The great novels will allow you to live more than one life.

—*Mary G., 64, Omaha, Nebraska*

Finding fulfillment spiritually, emotionally, and vocationally is important to your well-being. You are accountable for your body and only you can guard it, guide it, and nurture it.

Embrace life, love life; learn to cope with pain and adversity with courage. Be resilient. Be kind and compassionate. Be yourself.

—*Beverly B., 73, Edina, Minnesota*

I strongly encourage self-knowledge, for only as we know and understand ourselves can we know and understand others. Also aspire to acceptance and forgiveness of self. Only as we accept and forgive ourselves can we accept and forgive others. Finally, I recommend taking care of oneself in body, mind, and spirit (being one's own best friend). Listen to the "voice within." Mix together with HONESTY and the ability to communicate clearly with respect.

—*Gerri V., 49, Plymouth, Minnesota*

Keep a keen sense of humor; it will help you in many different situations and make you a more delightful person. When you are tempted to follow the crowd, believe in yourself. Be firm and don't be afraid to be "different". Everyone admires an individual who has principles and stands up to be counted. Act and do what you espouse because your credibility is in question. Be careful about what you want . . . you may get it!

Life is always good and sometimes it's better! Be an optimist. Life is better when the glass is half full!

—*Dodie P., 61, Ottawa, Canada*

It's crucial to know yourself, your strengths as much as your weaknesses, in order to develop your own beliefs and philosophy about life. Always be honest with yourself, how you feel, what you do, and your motives. Respect yourself so you can respect others. Be thoughtful about commitments so you can keep them to yourself as well as others. Have good friends, animal and human, and make time for them, enjoy them. Listen to others, but weigh their input with your inner voice. Take small steps (and keep taking them) and big ones too. Have fun, and enjoy your life; it's the only one you can live.

—*Pat L., 67, Princeton, Kentucky*

Learn how to give and take in order to live as peacefully as you can. Peace within is the best happiness we can achieve.

—*Leona H., 71, Billings, Montana*

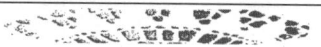

Learn to like yourself and learn from your mistakes. Be a role model and take very good care of your reputation. Have self-respect and be self-disciplined. Never compromise your integrity. Know the value of family!

—*Penny B., 54, Irving, Texas*

A positive attitude will help you through difficult times and make life better for you and others. Only you can control your attitude. Be honest with yourself as well as with others. Your friends will play an important part in your life so select them carefully. The way you live your life can make a difference; caring and kindness are contagious. God made you unique and special, and He loves you no matter what you do.

—*Eileen J., 61, Red Wing, Minnesota*

Life is a superb gift from God; treasure it! Make the most of every day and every opportunity. Each day is precious and filled with promise. Be optimistic, look for the "golden lining" in every cloud that temporarily hovers over you. Be loving and giving; all that you send into the life of others comes back into your own.

—*Harriet B., 72, Lake Park, Minnesota*

Have confidence in yourself and don't be afraid to fail; sometimes you learn from your failures.

—*LaVonne H., 61, Moorhead, Minnesota*

Life is like a play; you have the leading role. Make it an Oscar performance.

—*Kathie J., 49, Little Canada, Minnesota*

Life is not always a bed of roses. Learn to accept the disappointments or things you cannot change, but stand tall and be proud of what you are.

—*Wilma H., 69, Tulare, South Dakota*

Live life to the fullest. Do not pass up interesting opportunities. Do not be afraid to take chances. Learn from experience. Never look back, and say, "If only I had done this."

Life is a challenge; roll with the punches and take a deep breath and try again. Face reality and do not mourn what is past and can never be regained. Like yourself and what you do. Have pride in yourself.

—*Maryona J., 71, Miles City, Michigan*

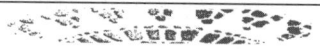

Live life with a positive attitude. There are a lot of changes in life, such as when you leave home. Just be yourself; it's the way God made you. Dare to be different from others. It is very fulfilling. Learn to control your own body and mind, and you will become a real person and genuinely independent. Don't act on impulse, but think things through. Make good choices.

—*Irene S., 56, Rothsay, Minnesota*

My greatest hope for you is that you have acquired self esteem. Self esteem is one of the most important assets, along with high morals and ethical standards, to get you through life. Self esteem is the very essence of being able to carry on when everything else around you seems to be falling apart.

—*Mona R., 62, Shakopee, Minnesota*

Only you can determine what kind of a life you will lead, so make it meaningful. I am so very proud of you; therefore, I will put all my trust in you.

You have this one life, so fill it with all the joy and happiness you can. Be true to yourself and do not sell yourself short.

—*Helen B., 83, Roseville, Minnesota*

Reflect on your life. You thereby have a tool for strengthening yourself. Reflect also on God. Knowledge of God is not frozen. Read, listen, reflect. Align yourself with others who do this. It is better to love and suffer the pain of loss than to insulate yourself from others.

—*Betty M., 64, Rochester, Minnesota*

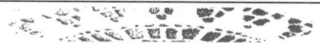

Remain true to yourself. Remember every tough situation you weather makes you stronger. Maintain a good sense of humor and laugh a lot, especially at yourself. Laughter makes living much more enjoyable.

—*Sharon D., 52, Washburn, Wisconsin*

Remember that character, dignity, and dependability are vital in life. Face your problems squarely and don't leave them for a later day or for someone else to solve for you. Live each day as though it were your last, because sometimes opportunities do not come your way again.

—*Norma T., 84, Reno, Nevada*

Smile. It's infectious.

—*Patricia N., 52, Fridley, Minnesota*

Take care of your whole self and encourage others to do the same.

—*Jane H., 67, St. Paul, Minnesota*

Take personal responsibility for your actions,
your needs, and solutions to your problems.
Things will get better. What happens to you is
less important than your reaction to events.
Make no major decisions at night. Joy, optimism
and courage come with the morning. Happiness
is your choice. Feel gratitude, feel it; thank God
and your special guardian angels,
family, and friends.

*—Becky Ann S., 73, West Lafayette,
Indiana*

The advice I have for my grandchildren is to live
your life as if everything you do will be on the
front page of the newspaper. Have faith and love
for your fellow man. Be determined and set
examples for your own children.
Show kindness to all.

—Leta C., 69, Midland, Michigan

The path to peace, joy, and love is by being true to your inner self. This means loving your whole self, totally, just as you are. "To love your neighbor as yourself" is the highest commandment God gives us. Don't forget that if you don't truly love who you are, you can't give much love to your neighbor, either. So you see, it starts by loving yourself, and multiplies by sharing that love with others. Unconditional love brings a joyous energy that will surely bless your life in peace. The strength of this calmness brings inner peace, right back full circle to where it all began.

—*Lois V., 53, Clear Lake, Wisconsin*

Be honest and fair with yourself, as well as with others. Set short-term goals first, with long-term expectations. Don't be disappointed if you have to make adjustments. Life is full of adjustments and you have to learn to be flexible. Have a good attitude and be happy.

—*Bonnie P., 53, Seattle, Washington*

You are liable for your own actions (right or wrong) and happiness. Don't fault someone else when things go wrong. This also pertains to boredom, there are things to do such as hobbies, volunteering, sports, and so on. Develop interests and you will not be bored nor without friends. Your parents have done the best for you that they could at the time so don't place blame (or guilt) on them for your mistakes or possible unhappiness.

—*Martha B., 71, Charlotte, Michigan*

Everything you do, think, or say is very important. It does not matter what other people think about you. You know who you are and you know that you are very special. God loves you and I love you.

—*Pat D., 56, Mission, Texas*

You will get out of life what you put into it.
I have several "rules of life:"

<u>Accentuate the positive</u>. Look for the good in all situations, there is always some there. Concentrate on the good and play down the bad.

<u>Do what comes naturally</u>. Remember your roots. It's good to improve yourself, but never think that you are better than anyone else. Perhaps you were just lucky to have had better opportunities.

<u>Keep it simple</u>. Life is not meant to be complicated; people make it so. The simple things in life are best!

—Karlene S., 58, Holyoke, Massachusetts

Your Great Grandfather always told me that it takes a lifetime to build a good name, but one mistake to ruin it.

—*Dorothy S., 71, Menomonie, Wisconsin*

I would like to have you experience your uniqueness. There is no one else on earth who has your combination of qualities. No one else on earth can make your observation, can give your insights. Respond with personal pride to every situation and every event. "Best" means giving whatever it is you can give.

—*Vivian L., 72, Mora, Minnesota*

Love, From Grandma

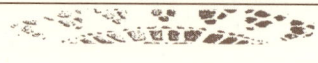

Take care of your family & friends.
Love,
Grandma

Treasure your family; they'll be there for you all your life.

—*Prudence B., 55, Rhinelander, Wisconsin*

Know that your family loves you and that you can always go home, even if it's only in your memories.

—*Judy R., 47, Breckenridge, Minnesota*

Always try to communicate with your parents; they are smarter than you think. Loyalty to family and your country is very important.

—*Marge D., 57, Reynolds, Indiana*

Be grateful to your parents; raising a child is not an easy task.

—*Alexia L., 63, Cleveland, Ohio*

Think before you act. Do not rush into relationships.

—*Helen H., 75, Chattanooga, Tennessee*

Before you commit to a life's partner, deal with the hard issues (both eyes and mind open) of spirituality and life's goals. Unfortunately, most often the differences will manifest themselves in "materialism" (it's a thing upon which one can hang one's gripe!). Travel not with a partner too attached to the material aspects of life; fortunes can change within a second.

—*Jo G., 56, Red Lodge, Montana*

Choose a lifetime partner with a similar family background, values, and goals. The same sort of church background is very helpful; if you differ, discuss your differences and their importance to you before marriage. Compromise will work with dedication. Be prepared for disagreement and try for resolution; don't run away at the first obstacle. Living together before marriage is not a commitment but a "cop-out," and does not necessarily lead to a long and happy marriage.

—*Martha B., 71, Charlotte, Michigan*

Don't jump into relationships; don't sleep around; always use protection.

—*Esther M., 66, South St. Paul, Minnesota*

Don't prepare so much for your wedding that you lose sight of the marriage.

—*Barbara M., 64, Mound, Minnesota*

Family and friends should be very important to you in your everyday life.

—*Jean K., 69, Fort Dodge, Iowa*

Family is important. Enjoy the holidays together and other special moments.

—*Sherrill P., 51, West St. Paul, Minnesota*

Help others. Keep up your religion and prayer life. Marry the right person and enjoy life.

—*Jewell K., 81, Lynnfield, Massachusetts*

It's just as easy to fall in love with a rich man as a poor one.

—*Florence B., 81, Rhinelander, Wisconsin*

Keep close to your family through letters, telephones, and visits. They love you and you want to nurture that love.

—*Lillian J., 77, Grand Forks, North Dakota*

Keep family ties strong. You need your independence, but a close family circle can help you through the tough times and give you great joy.

—*Judy F., 58, Wolcott, Indiana*

Find the best man or woman for your spouse; that is the most important thing you can do. Find someone of the same culture, heritage, and background with a stable family and interests.

—*Bernice J., 85, San Diego, California*

"Riches" do not mean money alone. Family, friendships, and health are riches to be desired more than money. Envying others (even siblings) for what they have can destroy you and your relationships with them. Try to make the best of what you have and what life deals to you. Remember that your family is still here for support and advice, if requested.

You are not alone.

—*Shirley R., 69, Dayton, Ohio*

Say "I love you" to those you do love.

—*Beatrice W., 61, Coon Rapids, Minnesota*

Treat your parents with respect and don't forget to be proud of where you came from.

—*LaVonne H., 61, Moorhead, Minnesota*

Value your family and friends, and call your grandmother once a week!

—*Charlotte D., 59, Dayton, Ohio*

I first would want my example of living life, my walk before my five grandchildren, to be more than my talk. Actions really do speak louder than words. I believe that children are a reflection of their parents and grandchildren are the blessings. The reward of a job well done. We all need someone to follow, someone to look up to; that's the privilege of being a grandmother.

Your family should be the most important thing in your life.

—*Gloria W., 68, Franklin Lakes, New Jersey*

When dating, always question whether you could be proud, happy, loving, and secure in life with a potential spouse. Looks and popularity are not the most important. Love, sincerity, and commitment are! Be selective and realistic.

—Jan A., 58, Prescott, Arizona

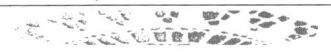

First and foremost, let your children know you
love them. Spoil and enjoy them from
infancy to adulthood.
Be firm with discipline, explain why if necessary.
Try to do projects (recreation, homework, cooking)
even when your children are very young. Mine
have always helped make bread, cookies, and so
on. We mixed meatloaf and shaped meatballs
(even though they were not always perfectly
round). Always praise their efforts,
no matter how minor.
Keep their imagination alive.
Children love to hear stories of the old days.
It never ceases to amaze me even the youngest
remember the tales; sometimes the stories are
true and sometimes make-believe. I've lived in
the North Shore of Lake Superior, a wilderness in
the 20's and early 30's. Children love to hear
adventures of those days.

*—Elizabeth T., 69, St. Clair Shores,
Michigan*

Love, From Grandma

Take care of others.
Love,
Grandma

Accept, encourage, allow, support and relish how different we all are, one from another.

—*Judy A., 56, Baldwin, New York*

Always be honest and open. Have good communication with others. Treat all people with respect regardless of race or income. Remember that you are as good as any person, yet don't feel that you are better than anyone.

Always have faith in yourself and faith in the Lord, and you will always have hope and anything that you pursue will be possible.

Love yourself; don't depend on others to make you happy.

—*Irene H., 69, Avon, Minnesota*

Have compassion instead of rebellion, understanding instead of judgment and above all, love and caring.

Always remember to respect people for themselves and not for what they can do for you.

—*Elizabeth S., 70, Kamuela, Hawaii*

If, throughout your life, you help feed the hungry, clothe the poor, visit the sick, bury the dead, you will be a wonderful friend and have many friends. And that is what life is all about. You will be living each day to the fullest and have a beautiful life.

—*Mona R., 62, Shakopee, Minnesota*

Be giving and forgiving. Seek out the good in people and love unconditionally. Be in control of your life, but don't try to control others.

—*Penny B., 54, Irving, Texas*

Be honest. Set high morals for yourself. Be considerate of others, give of yourself, care for people. Use good manners always.

—*LaVonne H., 61, Moorhead, Minnesota*

Be kind to everyone, especially older people.

—*Dorothy H., 82, Bemidji, Minnesota*

If you find yourself in an unpleasant or harmful situation, leave or get out NOW! Do not let unkind thoughts become unkind words.

—Patricia B., 55, Palmer, Alaska

Trust your instincts; trust your judgment about people. Never be cruel. Love all the creatures of the world. Love others as if they were you. Love yourself.

—Lee C., 74, Munich, Germany

Be loving and caring with people; we are God's children. Care for creation and the gifts we have been given; they are ours to borrow and pass on to others in better condition than we found them, if possible.

—Carolyn C., 61, Crystal, Minnesota

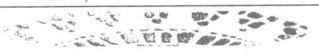

Be loyal to your friends and keep a sense of humor. It helps with life's downs. Don't let silly misunderstandings cause major problems with friends or fellow workers. Life is not always fair, so you must be strong and not be afraid to seek help. Be kind and try to see both sides of a problem. Above all, my dear grandchild, know that you are loved and keep in touch.

—Dorothy G., 70, Northville, Michigan

Be open to all new possibilities. Don't be afraid to listen to those who differ from you or your past experiences.

—Marie G., 71, Lamberton, Minnesota

Be quick to say "I'm sorry" when you are to blame, and mean it! Be slow to judge others, for as you judge, so you will be judged.
Be honest in all your dealings.

—Agnes B., 84, San Jose, California

Be respectful of others as to their feelings, space, and belongings.

—*Patricia N., 52, Fridley, Minnesota*

Be yourself; don't try to be someone you are not. Have love and understanding for all people regardless of race or religion. Aim high. You can be anything you want, just be honest, sincere, dependable, and a good friend to all your friends.

—*Gwen M., 69, Hampton, New Hampshire*

Don't waste your time or energy on hatred, bigotry, anger, or worry. Believe in the energizing power of love, and don't take yourself too seriously.

—*Janet W., 86, Naples, Florida*

Listen. . .Listen to one another intently with your whole being. Listen with your heart. Listen with your eyes. Listen with your ears. Shut down your inner voice when you actively listen.
Close off your barriers of thoughts, feelings, opinions, and advice. Focus your attention to the listening gift you freely give.

—*Louise O., 49, Minneapolis, Minnesota*

Do not focus on one aspect of your life nor a single individual. Enjoy all the gifts of life: nature, the arts, literature, food, but most of all enjoy the people—family, friends, community and the chance acquaintance. Listen, listen to what they say, respect their thoughts, think upon them, and you will travel in mind and spirit throughout the universe.

—*Jo G., 56, Red Lodge, Montana*

Don't always think about yourself. What you give in return will make you feel much happier.

—*Shirley P., 70, Roseville, Minnesota*

Don't be afraid to love or to show love.

—*Eileen J., 61, Red Wing, Minnesota*

Fill yourself with love, grace, warmth, and sensitivity, and become a recycler of them all. Always be loyal. Once a friend, always a friend. Somehow, when we meet disloyalty, it is never forgotten. Do something for someone else every day of your life and preferably on the "Q. T." And patience—what a gift! Be kind, thoughtful, and generous, but don't increase your stress by being too nice.

Just be yourself. You're wonderful!!
When you encounter someone with a lack of graciousness, kill them with kindness and then avoid them like the plague!

Keep your sense of humor. Remember, God wants us to love others, but we certainly don't have to like them! <u>Love</u> unconditionally, but <u>like</u> at your own gait.

—*Gracie G., 67, Alpena, Michigan*

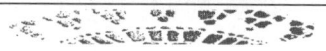

Go with the greater love. Treat other people as you would like them to treat you. Care for people's feelings. We are all in process. To accept myself and others means to accept a house in the making.

—Betty M., 64, Rochester, Minnesota

Have compassion for all people and all creatures. Give a thought to those of us who walked the road before you.

—Allegra V., 70, Midland, Michigan

Manners are very important and will help you all your life. A smile and a friendly manner, plus a genuine "thank you" can save the day! Be very cautious, though; don't be gullible, and be sure to pay attention to your surroundings and the people around you!

—Ida K., 69, St. Paul, Minnesota

Live each day to its fullest by being honest and kind to all people. Be fair; don't treat others like you do not want to be treated yourself. Trust in the Lord always. Help and respect others. I feel that we get out of life what we put into it.

—Judy S.C., 54, Anoka, Minnesota

Here is my favorite quote: "Caution, human beings here, handle with care!" You don't have to love, or even like, everyone you meet, but you do need to give them the respect and dignity that they deserve as children of God.

—Sandy L., 46, Plymouth, Minnesota

If you treat others with honor and fairness, with a disposition that is kind and forgiving while remaining aware of your own strengths and weaknesses, you will have a solid foundation on which to build infinite relationships with other human beings.

—Norma H., 69, Lenox, Massachusetts

In helping others, any little gesture on your part can mean so much. If you follow the "Golden Rule" you will have acquired a great understanding of others.

—*Helen B., 83, Roseville, Minnesota*

Keep in contact with friends and family that are important to you; know that those people are there to support you in any way that you need. Make new friends, too, to enrich and broaden your life and theirs.

—*Carol P., 56, Harrisville, Rhode Island*

Show kindness to others who need your help and guidance. Be a caring person full of love.

—*Beverly T., 55, Acton, Massachusetts*

Learn from the mistakes and experiences of others as well as your own.

—*Mary D., 53, Peoria, Illinois*

Learn to get along with your fellow human beings. Loving, caring, and sharing are apt watchwords of life.

—*Beverly B., 73, Edina, Minnesota*

Let yourself be God's instrument of God's love for all humankind.

—*Marianne W., 63, St. Paul, Minnesota*

Live your life as a helpful person. Be loving, forgiving, and helpful at all times.

—*Lillian L., 78, Baltimore, Maryland*

Live your life with a positive attitude and surround yourself with positive people. Treat everyone you come in contact with, young or old, with kindness and an open mind. Treat other people and other people's property the way you would want to be treated.

—*Edith G., 64, Methuen, Massachusetts*

Learn to know people of many races, religions, and cultures, and appreciate their uniqueness.

Share your ideas, dreams, times, talents, and material goods.

Develop your ability to be a friend, to be caring and supportive.

Above all, give God the glory in all good things that come your way.

—*Mae Lou T., 59, Beresford, South Dakota*

Love, caring, and relationships with people are more important than accumulating "things". Things can't make you happy. You make your own happiness.

—*Mary C., 56, Hudson, Wisconsin*

Make friends and enjoy your friendships, but don't be enthralled by them.

—*Mary S., 69, Burnsville, Minnesota*

Never go against your good judgment and follow a peer or group in the wrong direction. It could prove to be very expensive and possibly ruin your entire life. Be strong, do right, and enjoy a successful life. Be considerate of others, especially the less fortunate. Be willing to lend a helping hand to family, neighbors, and friends. Be a good listener, never boastful.

—*Thestina T., 83, Grand Forks, North Dakota*

Put honesty and fair play above lying, cheating, and greed. Have a vital interest in what is happening around you, and try to make this world a little better place by what you do.

—Norma T., 84, Reno, Nevada

Regardless of how folks (family and friends) treat you, think of how you would like to be treated and follow that path.

—Ethel S., 74, Woodbury, Connecticut

Seek God, love God, love yourself; then you can love others. Each day do something for, or give something to, another in SECRET. Do unto others as you would have them do unto you.

If "everyone is doing it"— don't.
Think! Think! Think!

—Becky Ann S., 73, West Lafayette, Indiana

Something a nun passed on to me: "Only God can judge you, not your neighbors."

—*Carmen K., 60, Shoreview, Minnesota*

Take support from your family and be there for them. Happiness comes from being concerned for the welfare of others. Don't be selfish!!

—*Jean K., 69, Fort Dodge, Iowa*

Remember those who are hurting and reach out to them in appropriate ways.

—*Marlys S., 69, Sun City West, Arizona*

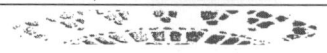

Show love, patience, and compassion. It is in giving, not getting, that our lives are blessed. Remember life worth living is giving and forgiving. Also a sharp tongue causes friction but loving words promote peace and harmony.

Always be a good listener.

—*Ruth R., 87, Fort Dodge, Iowa*

The more you give of yourself, the more you receive in return in all aspects of your life. Think before you speak. Be kind and, above all else, don't be judgmental. Unkind and hurtful words last a lifetime. Saving face is less important than saving a friendship. Enjoy yourself, but never at someone else's expense. We are in a diverse and interesting world. All people are God's children. Be open and inquiring to learn more because we never stop learning. Bring your hurts and pain home to those who love you. Never say never, because those who really love you will be there for you.

—*Dodie P., 61, Ottawa, Canada*

There's "good" in every person if we only will take the time, love, and concern to find it and help them.

—*Wilma H., 69, Tulare, South Dakota*

To have a friend, you must be one. Friends of all ages make life interesting. Laugh and have fun. It is not necessary to have alcohol or drugs to have fun. Be responsible for your actions.

Do something for others. There are so many good causes and so few people volunteer.

—*Lillian J., 77, Grand Forks, North Dakota*

Be more charitable than today's generation. The world today seems to have many self-indulgent people. They are sometimes violent and have little respect for life. (We're all here for a purpose and that is to love your neighbor as yourself.)

—*Mary L., 65, Chicago, Illinois*

Try not to be gullible or naive in your relationships, social as well as professional.

—*Shirley R., 69, Dayton, Ohio*

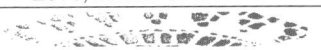

Treat others as you wish to be treated. Be honest and open with people, work hard and apply yourself, but don't forget to enjoy life and people. Try to see something positive in each and every person you come in contact with.
Expose yourself to all walks of life and you will be a terrific adult.

—Dorothy B., 58, St. Paul, Minnesota

Try to walk in someone else's shoes to see how he or she feels.

—LaVonne H., 61, Moorhead, Minnesota

We only get one chance in this lifetime and we should give it our best shot. Live life to the fullest but without hurting anyone else in doing so. Be kind, generous, and considerate of everyone you meet along life's way.

—Adele P., 60, St. Paul, Minnesota

Love, From Grandma

Take care of your spirit. Love, Grandma

Nurture your spiritual health even more than your physical health. Seek God, love God, love yourself; then you can love others. Believe in the triumph of good always. Express gratitude to family, friends, associates, and God.

> —*Becky Ann S., 73, West Lafayette, Indiana*

Keep God in your life because with God all things are possible. Keep prayer in your life and read inspirational material.

> —*Marion D-H., 50, Knoxville, Tennessee*

Say your prayers every day. Your strong faith in God can pull you through the darkest of times.

> —*Patricia B., 55, Palmer, Alaska*

Prayer changes things. Trust in the Lord.

> —*Ruth R., 87, Fort Dodge, Iowa*

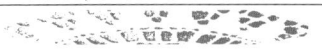

We were all made by the same God and He loves us all equally. Can we do any less? Love your God, love your family, love your fellowman, and it will follow that you will love yourself.

—Karlene S., 58, Holyoke, Massachusetts

Seek self-esteem tempered by respect for others and an abiding faith in a loving God who created all things. An attitude of love for ourselves, our neighbors, and our God is the basis for happiness and well-being in body, mind, and spirit. Such balance and inner peace comes as a gift from God. Choose Jesus, the way of love, and you choose not only the abundant life but eternal life.

—Marj C., 73, Atwood, Kansas

We need not blunder through life following only our whims. God will be with you in decision-making. Dare to be guided by the Holy Spirit.

—Gerda L., 78, Albion, Nebraska

Remember, God wants us to love others, but we don't have to like them!

—Gracie G., 67, Alpena, Michigan

Keep God active in your life.

—Judy F., 58, Wolcott, Indiana

If you start your day with prayer, God will lead
and guide you. Remember, God is on call
24 hours a day.

—Arleen K., 70, Thompson, North Dakota

Think highly of yourself and stay close to God.
You will have good friends and be able to
resist temptation.

—Elizabeth W., 78, Sebastian, Florida

Always carry God's love with you. It will enable
you to understand and to forgive. Appreciate all
that God has given you.

—Ruth C., 76, Sioux Falls, South Dakota

It gives you a good feeling to go to church.

—Dorothy H., 82, Bemidji, Minnesota

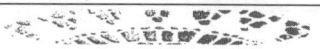

You are a child of a loving God and have inherent and infinite worth.

—*Christina S., 75, Spokane, Washington*

Life is a gift, in all forms, through God. If life seems too complicated, return to your childhood faith. You will see the right path to take.

—*Muriel O., 67, Thompson, North Dakota*

Everyone you meet is made in God's image. Give them the respect and the dignity they deserve as children of God. Nurture your own relationship with God. Spiritual nurturing is every bit as important as physical and mental nurturing.

—*Sandy L., 46, Plymouth, Minnesota*

As a child of God your priorities should be: Daily Devotions, Prayer and Praise, 10% Tithe, and Weekly Worship.

—*Elaine K., 62, Cottage Grove, Minnesota*

Stay close to the Lord; He'll give you guidance and wisdom. You have to take time to receive it. If you do, there will be no challenge in your life that His counsel cannot solve.

—*Helen B., 71, Minneapolis, Minnesota*

Develop a strong spiritual life. It will ease the problems and difficulties of life, and enhance the joys and successes. Spirituality allows you to accept and love yourself; until you love yourself you cannot love another as a friend or lover.

—*Jo G., 56, Red Lodge, Montana*

Love God, love and care for yourself, your family, and others — in this order. If you truly love God and yourself, everything else will fall into place.

—*Kathy P., 55, New Market, Alabama*

Take time to be quiet and talk to God. Enjoy the beauty of creation and preserve it. Above all, give God the glory in all good things that come your way.

—Mae Lou T., 59, Beresford, South Dakota

God made you unique and special, one of a kind, and He loves you no matter what you do.

—Eileen J., 61, Red Wing, Minnesota

Walk with God. Life is difficult, and He has much to teach as you walk through and grow because of those hard times.

—Gerry L., 56, Grand Forks, North Dakota

The best advice I can give is to have faith, hope, and charity. Have Faith in God, a personal relationship with our living Savior, and faith in yourself. Have Hope for the future and a positive approach to everything. And have Charity, to share of yourself with others, to give help to those who are in need, and to share your talents.

—*Olive B., 61, Hatton, North Dakota*

"Seek ye first the Kingdom of God and all things will be added."

—*Clara A., 81, Brooklyn Center, Minnesota*

God's love is ours always.

—*Jackie O., 50, Dawson, Minnesota*

Life is a superb gift from God; treasure it! Make the most of every day and every opportunity.

—*Harriet B., 72, Lake Park, Minnesota*

Attend Sunday School and Church. Believe in God. He will keep you on the right path and help you through all your trials and tribulations.

—*Beatrice W., 61, Coon Rapids, Minnesota*

Reflect on God. Knowledge of God is not frozen. Read, listen, pray, think. Align yourself with others who do this.

—*Betty M., 64, Rochester, Minnesota*

If you make mistakes, ask God to forgive you, and accept that you are forgiven. Put a high value on yourself. You are as God made you.

—*Irene S., 56, Rothsay, Minnesota*

Place spiritual values above everything.

—*Eleanor B., 72, Golden Valley, Minnesota*

Become acquainted with your God. Talk to Him as you walk, dream, or pray. He listens, whether you call him Jesus, Budda, or Jehovah.

—*Allegra V., 70, Midland, Michigan*

Live life fully each day for God. Greet each day with the prayer, "Lord, what are you and I going to do together today? I'm reporting for duty." You'll never be bored.

—*Pearl S., 61, Houston, Texas*

There is only one answer to life and living. It is found in the Bible, in Proverbs 3:5-6. I paraphrase: We need to trust in the Lord with all our heart, and not rely on our own human fallible understanding. We should in all our ways acknowledge Him as our Supreme God, and then we will know that He will direct our paths.

—*Louise W., 62, Hollidaysburg, Pennsylvania*

Always take joy in the little things God gives you, along with His greater gifts. Don't keep your relationship with God too sacred. Talk to Him when you're in the shower or stuck in traffic.

—*Judy R., 47, Breckenridge, Minnesota*

Always think of yourself as loved by God, Who is Love.

—*Margaret Mary M., 69, Morris, Minnesota*

Treasure honesty, both in listening to the Spirit within and in dealing with all peoples. Build a strong and personal relationship with your God. Do all you can to deepen that bond of love and trust between the Creator and yourself. Have no fear where that leads; let yourself be God's instrument of love for all humankind.

—*Marianne W., 63, St. Paul, Minnesota*

Go to church and find friends through church. Try to find a good community to live in. Start out if possible in a place where you have friends or relatives.

—*Marion M., 74, Canby, Oregon*

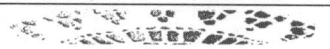

When you were born you became a gift to your family. You are a special child of God.

—Pat D., 66, Mission, Texas

God loves you and I love you.

—Ella B., 61, Trondheim, Norway

We are God's workmanship!

—Mary D., 50, Carrollton, Texas

Micah 6:8 says, "He hath showed thee, O Man, what is good and what doth the Lord require of thee, but to be just, and to love mercy, and to walk humbly with thy God?" The prophet wrote these words centuries ago, and I offer them to you as a touchstone. If you treat others with honor and fairness, with a disposition that is kind and forgiving, while remaining aware of your own strengths and weaknesses, you will have a solid foundation on which to build infinite relationships with other human beings. Count each day as a new beginning, the first day of the rest of your life. Show reverence for God.

—Norma H., 69, Lenox, Massachusetts

Love, From Grandma

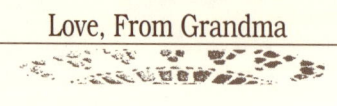

Take care of your future.
Love,
Grandma

Be happy at what you intend to do.

—*Wilma H., 69, Tulare, South Dakota*

1. Be clear about who you are and why you are here.
2. Have fun every day.
3. Learn from everything you do.
4. Ask plenty of questions.

—*Betsy B., 47, Duluth, Minnesota*

Always save a percent of your income regardless how small the amount. Tomorrow always comes; the sun keeps rising and setting.

—*Flo E., 55, Bismarck, North Dakota*

Be happy when someone else wins the race, the game, the money.

—*Cathy C., 53, Minnetonka, Minnesota*

Be cheerful and friendly to people. Have good work ethics; show up for work, and be on time. Don't stand around and gossip; try to keep busy. Have good people skills and communication skills. Young people should be "well," not always calling in sick at the latest hour. Obtain an education that will support you in your life. Computer skills are important in this day and age. Do not chew gum at work.

—*Agnes S., 83, Cavalier, North Dakota*

Be honest and considerate, it will gain you the trust of others. Without it you have nothing. Money won't buy you happiness only a few material comforts. Friends, family, and time for yourself should come before work.

—*Sandra G., 51, Princeton, Minnesota*

Work hard at whatever job or endeavor you choose. Do not undertake more than you can handle whether that should be commitments or credit.

—Jane H., 65, St. Paul, Minnesota

Complete your education. Be independent. Just 'cause you get married doesn't mean that he will support you.

—Esther M., 66, South St. Paul, Minnesota

Count each day as a new beginning, the first day of the rest of your life, while remembering to show reverence for your God.

—Norma H., 69, Lenox, Massachusetts

If you truly want to be successful in your career, you must pursue it vigorously, most likely making sacrifices. If family life is more important to you, realize that you must focus your actions on that.

—*Jean K., 71, St. Petersburg, Florida*

Don't expect the "good life" to be handed to you on a silver platter. Earn it by preparing yourself for life by getting a good education. Have goals and do your utmost to achieve them. Don't squander anything; your health, your resources, or the good old common sense you inherited. Don't take any of the above for granted. They are priceless. You can't buy them for any price. They are God's gift to you. You didn't earn them but you are obligated to share with those less fortunate than you.

—*Gladys S., 87, Grand Forks, North Dakota*

Since a great deal of your time will be spent at your job, make the most of it. Do your fair share, be on time, don't whine and complain, be neat and clean. Be kind to those less fortunate than yourself. Your rewards will be many.

—*Kay F., 52, Staples, Minnesota*

Don't waste away your life on a good time, but always think where your actions will lead you. Yes, THINK. God gave you a good mind; use it.

—*Viola R., 73, Petersburg, Nebraska*

Know your craft and do it better than the others.

—*Geraldine H., 78, Kansas City, Missouri*

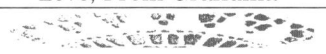

Make the most of your opportunities. Education is very important, although college isn't always possible. There are many technical schools that will help you train for a career. Look into grants and scholarships early. Do your best and have fun doing it.

—*Ruth S., 82, Preston, Minnesota*

It is not necessary to have a lot of money. Money and power do not make us happy. They only make us want more.

—*Lillian J., 77, Grand Forks, North Dakota*

Life is a wonderful thing. It is up to each of us to take care of our lives. We are given ability. As an adult you must choose how you are going to live your life and know right from wrong. You have to apply yourself to reach a goal, a goal you'd like to achieve.

—*Ruth M., 83, Auburn, Washington*

Develop a positive attitude and expect to achieve success. Your attitudes are self-fulfilling. Having a positive attitude will help you be successful.

—*Ginger J., 57, Portland, North Dakota*

Life is not necessarily meant to be easy and there is no guarantee that you will be "taken care of." Work hard and plan for your future, even into retirement. But set aside some time for fun and relaxation. It makes the rest easier. Keep God active in your life.

—*Judy F., 58, Wolcott, Indiana*

Life is the happiest and the most worthwhile if you savor planting the seeds, watching them grow, and nurturing them, not just picking the fruit and the flowers.

—*Barbara M., 64, Mound, Minnesota*

Life will have its trials, its ups and downs. With optimism, logic, and consideration of others, life can be very good.

—*Hildegard S., 64, Munich, Germany*

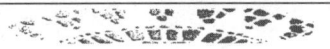

Live life NOW!!! Do all you can today with no financial debts! Spend only what you can afford.

—*Ruth B., 86, Woodmere, New York*

Most of us are eager to press forward in life. To do this we must be ambitious with a desire to control our own destiny.

—*Gerda L., 78, Albion, Nebraska*

Early in life, do jobs that will help you learn to manage money and get along with older people, so by the time you leave home you will have some idea of what to expect. No one owes you a living. The competition is getting greater in the workforce as the years go by, and money is harder to come by. Go to college as soon as you finish high school.

—*Ollie T., 65, Brownwood, Texas*

Live life to the fullest! Don't hold back.
Hold onto your dreams.
If you believe you can do it, you will.
Set goals and take a step each day toward those goals.

—*Marion D-H., 50, Knoxville, Tennessee*

My advice is to make the best of what you have, learn to handle your own money, and spend it wisely. Whatever you choose to do, do it well. Be fair in all dealings and business matters. Be a true friend, neighbor, and worker.

—*Irene H., 84, Casselton, North Dakota*

Never say "never." We have no idea what the future holds for us.

—*Ethel S., 74, Woodbury, Connecticut*

Set your own ethical standard and live up to it. Don't let others decide your future. Set your own courses and row towards them at all times.
Life is good. Bounce back. Remember, when you point at someone else, four fingers are pointing back at you. Experiment with life to expand your visions. Dare to care!

—*Frances S., 58, London, England*

The world you live in is full of opportunities to fulfill your every dream. You will be tempted in many ways, but follow your good common sense and don't be intimidated by people.

—*Dorothy S., 71, Menomonie, Wisconsin*

Be true to yourself and the principles that have been taught you. You have been well educated and are intelligent. Much is expected of people with your abilities, but with hope you will approach life as a great gift and have enormous fun and enjoyment. You are a reflection of the people who have loved and raised you.

—*Karleen P., 56, Hudson, Wisconsin*

Never waver in your pursuits. Reach for the stars; many things are possible. The road of life brings many unexpected hills and valleys. It is at these times that you must not swerve. Perhaps around the bend the road of life will again become straight.

—Frances R., 88, Holyoke, Massachusetts

When you fall for any reason, pick yourself up and start anew; with every fallback, you go forward to a better existence. Keep on learning, which is the key to a successful person. Keep busy and productive with hobbies and interests to insure yourself a rewarding retirement with many things to do when life is lonely.

—Patricia N., 52, Fridley, Minnesota

Youth is so impetuous. You must learn to accept things more readily. We can't have everything overnight. Work diligently and the rewards will begin to be seen. Remember your roots. Worship regularly as you were brought up in your Christian home. Slow down; Rome wasn't built in a day.

—S. Jeanette F., 68, Grand Forks, North Dakota

You have finally reached that point in your young life where you have only yourself to answer to. Sounds wonderful, doesn't it? Or does it feel a little scary? Remember, you have two of the most wonderful resources to turn to for help, encouragement, understanding, and most of all, love: your faith in God and your parents. When life gets "tough," they will be there for you.

—*Mary Ann Z., 60, Woodbury, Minnesota*

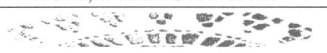

When we were children, we were so eager for life to get on with itself. Go slowly. Everything happens in its time. Life should not be fleeting. It should be slow, rich, and long (ideally so).

—*Kathie J., 49, Little Canada, Minnesota*

You are a very special person. Live each day to the fullest. You have been given a childhood filled with a generous amount of life. Continue to share, and love each day. Strive to be the best at whatever profession you may choose. Use your God-given talents and remember that no matter what your age, your grandparents will be there for you.

—*Lois W., 58, Columbus, Wisconsin*

I wish my training would have taught me early in life to set goals. You need short term and long term goals, not only in your career, but also personal and spiritual as well!

You'll encounter many people in your lifetime who will work hard to make you miss your targets. Remember, they're YOUR GOALS and only you can achieve them!

Regardless of your age, grade school and up, it's never too early to plan ahead. If you miss something, don't be discouraged. BOUNCE BACK! Re-evaluate, reorganize, and proceed!

Learn from your setbacks! It's not always the best for you to be the "winner." You will gain more strength, empathy, and insight if you're not always #1. You'll not be the first nor the last.

—*Jan A., 58, Prescott, Arizona*

Do what you want to do. Further your education no matter what occupation you choose. You may change your mind after studying awhile.

—*Helen O., 78, Preston, Minnesota*

Decide what you really want to do with your life.
Set goals to achieve goals.
First get a good education; if you can read,
you can accomplish anything!

—*Betty S., 69, Ponca City, Oklahoma*

Love, From Grandma

Take care of your values and beliefs.
Love,
Grandma

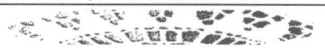

Always do what you think is right according to <u>your</u> heart. It is a constant. Society's views change constantly.

—*Jeanette S., 56, Monterey, California*

As much as possible, live by the Golden Rule and the Ten Commandments.

—*Jewell K., 81, Lynnfield, Massachusetts*

Be fair. Have good morals. Don't follow the crowd if it goes against your moral code. Don't be afraid to say no!!

—*Mary C., 61, Forest Lake, Minnesota*

Enduring values are better than pleasure for the moment.

—*Carolyn C., 61, Crystal, Minnesota*

Examine and define your values. Do not choose to do anything that violates your values. This includes issues such as employment, housing (where you live and who you live with), and who your friends are. Smaller decisions will come more easily once these big decisions are in place.

—*Myrna N., 55, Plankinton, South Dakota*

Family and friends are all important. Whatever your choices, consider how you will feel in later years. Be true to your own values. Be glad for life and opportunities and smell the flowers! Life is an exciting adventure; live it to the fullest!

—*Jean V., 70, Baldwin, Wisconsin*

Have good moral values and standards. Life makes sense only if we can relate it to lasting values.

—*Irene H., 69, Avon, Minnesota*

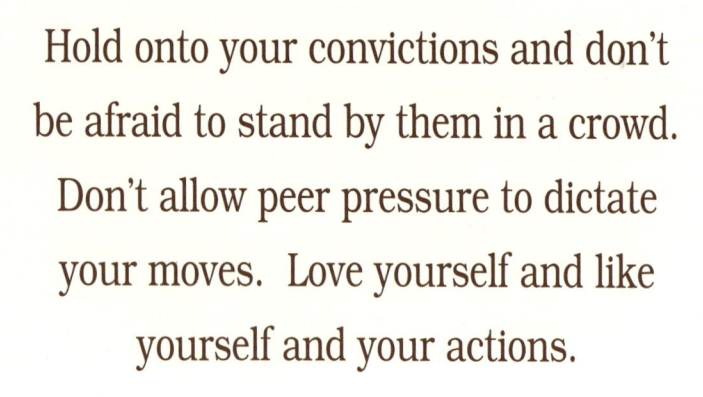

Hold onto your convictions and don't be afraid to stand by them in a crowd. Don't allow peer pressure to dictate your moves. Love yourself and like yourself and your actions.

—*Pat J., 58, Lake View, Iowa*

I believe in the old fashioned values of honesty, morality, compassion, reliability, and responsibility.

—*Martha B., 71, Charlotte, Michigan*

Keep your <u>word</u> at any cost.

—*Priscilla G., 47, Camarillo, California*

Let your conscience be your guide. Don't allow a friend to talk you into doing something you really don't want to do if you know it is wrong. You can say no; it is OK! Be your own person.

—*Beatrice W., 61, Coon Rapids, Minnesota*

Life is very short. Decide how you want to live it. Set your own values and direction, and go for it!

—*Mary C., 56, Hudson, Wisconsin*

Life today is much more of a challenge and trial than it was when I grew up. We weren't faced with all the temptations you have nowadays. It takes a much stronger person to say "no" than to follow the crowd. Our society is getting more permissive all the time. Set your goals high. "When the going gets tough, the tough get going" is a good motto.

—*Mildred S., 74, Grand Forks, North Dakota*

Don't let others make decisions for you. Because today's society is so culturally, morally, and economically diverse, we must always evaluate our beliefs carefully before making decisions. We must learn to understand and respect other's values, yet feel proud of our own heritage and values. Value "you" as a person.

—*E. Irene T., 68, New Hope, Minnesota*

Know and appreciate what is close to you and make your life worth living. Live each day as a gift. You can't get it back, but you'll have a chance tomorrow to do it over.

Try to pursue your innermost interests, but at the same time don't overlook the possibilities of a situation that could be promising.

Examine and re-examine and develop your friendships and family.

—*Marcella M., 77, Sioux City, Iowa*

My primary advice is "Don't procrastinate." Sloth (which includes procrastination) is a vastly underrated sin. Though not as much fun as some of the others, it is just as deadly.

—Elizabeth L., 78, St. Paul, Minnesota

Place spiritual values above everything.

—Eleanor B., 72, Golden Valley, Minnesota

Remember the moral standards you were raised with.

—Helen H., 75, Chattanooga, Tennessee

Stand up for what you believe.

—Carol P., 56, Harrisville, Rhode Island

Your values are very important; stick to them. Don't let anyone persuade you to do otherwise. Live life to the fullest.

—Shirley P., 70, Roseville, Minnesota

Values are hard to keep in perspective, but to me they make our lives what they are. They must be considered very carefully; values change with maturity. I pondered this one Sunday as I glanced around at people who had gathered for a church service, retirees who had moved South for the winter. People from all walks of life, from different parts of the country, many years ago, had to make the same decisions you are facing now. In my mind, as in many others, I'm sure, the things that seemed so important
really weren't.

The "words" of advice that I think would top my list are these: 1. <u>Unselfishness</u>. This is what "earns" love from family and gains you many friends. You can't live without them. 2. <u>Honesty</u>. So that when you are one of the oldies you'll not feel badly about hurting someone along the way. 3. <u>Faith</u>. This is the most important. There is Someone who cares very much about what happens to you.

—Marge B., 73, Austin, Minnesota

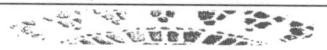

Appreciate your history, be glad you are an American, that your ancestors had the courage to leave their homes and come to America.

—*Prudence B., 55, Rhinelander, Wisconsin*

I recommend old fashioned morality based on teachings of the Bible.

—*Mary Jane B., 74, Chicago, Illinois*

Though it is nice to be well thought of and respected, don't cheat your own values and ideas just to gain someone else's acceptance of you. Be a leader when you can, but there is nothing wrong with being a follower.

—*Sharon K., 49, Chicago, Illinois*

Greet each day as a new, wonderful challenge and a precious gift. You don't have time for preoccupation with past negatives.

—*Pat S., 70, Largo, Florida*

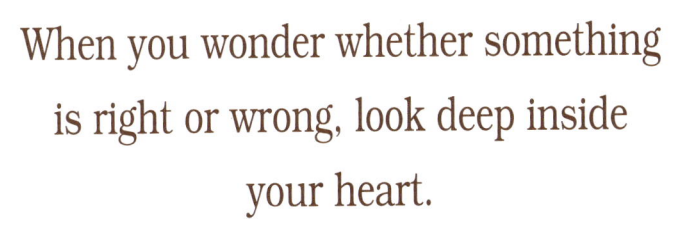

When you wonder whether something is right or wrong, look deep inside your heart.

—Lee C., 74, Munich, Germany

Love, From Grandma

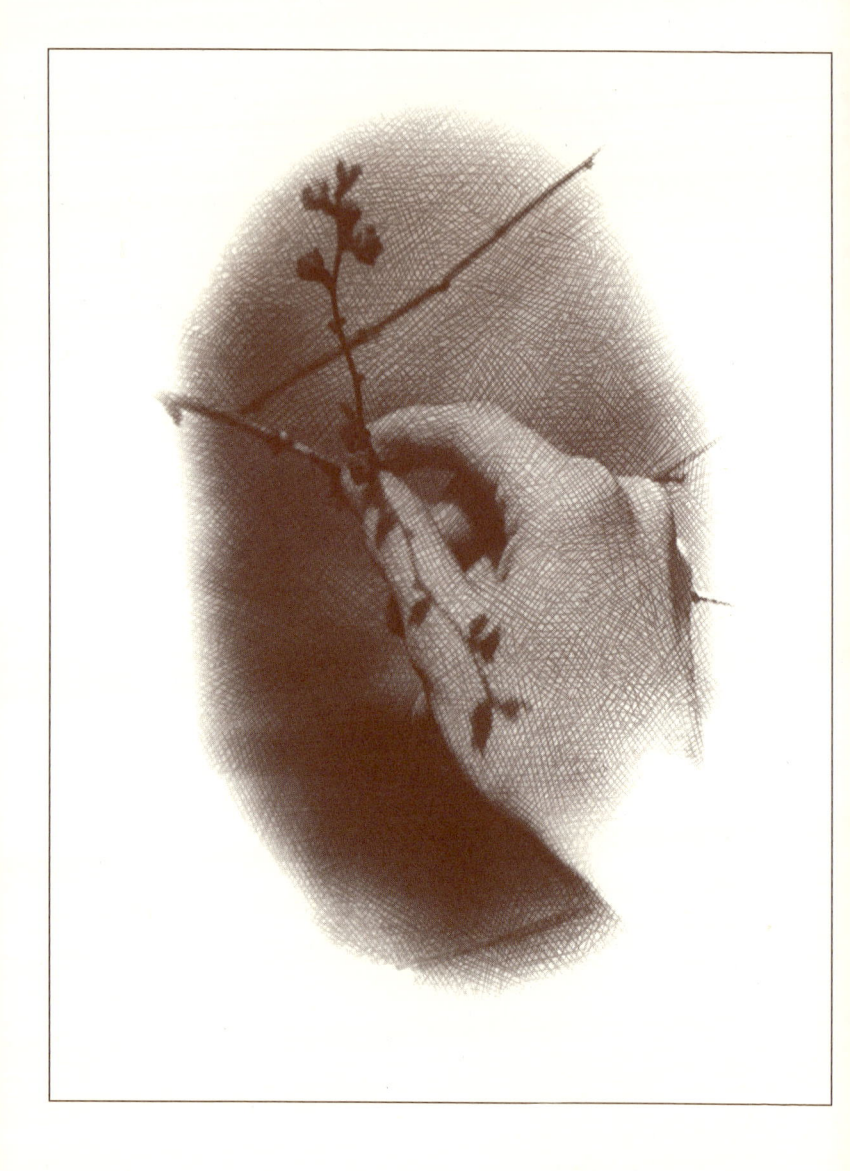

Take care of all the rest.
Love,
Grandma

Love, From Grandma

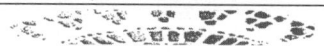

Always finish what you start.
Spend no more than you have.
Save 10%. Give 10%. (10/10/80 plan).
Remember, you are never alone.

—Betty H., 67, Nekoosa, Wisconsin

Always wear clean underwear in case you're in an accident.

—Florence B., 81, Rhinelander, Wisconsin

Be cautious, but not so much you don't take chances or have fun while living a full life. Be sure you give by volunteering. Do as much traveling as possible.

—Virginia M., 61, Dunwoody, Georgia

Do lots of reading. Cultivate a hobby or things to do when you're alone (e.g., reading). Do something fun for exercise and eat healthy foods. Nourish your spiritual life through books and prayer.

—Jeanne C., 73, St. Paul, Minnesota

Do several things well rather than being too scattered.

—*Jane H., 67, St. Paul, Minnesota*

Don't live for tomorrow. Enjoy each day to the fullest. Don't waste time on regrets or guilts. We all have them. Be truthful and never hide secrets that make you lie. They multiply. Focus on the wonderful things that you can experience every day.
Take time to notice all of the beauty around you and remember that this is a gift.

—*Allegra V., 70, Midland, Michigan*

Dress and act respectfully. Pick an appropriate neighborhood. Lock all doors and windows. Do not open doors to strangers. Remember your religion by going to church regularly. Pick your company. Keep your house and surroundings clean and neat. Open a savings account and save regularly in order to have funds for an emergency.

—*Julia B., 71, Pensacola, Florida*

Eat well and exercise.

Pleasure is necessary, but not all of life. It is good to know how to delay pleasure (e.g., do your homework first, then watch TV).

Pay attention to your dreams. They tell you what's going on in your unconsciousness, and can help you.

Do what you want, but be careful about this.

—*Betty M., 64, Rochester, Minnesota*

Enjoy life and get involved in several extracurricular activities.

Be conscious and responsible for your actions. Avoid the temptations of alcohol, drugs, smoking, and sex.

Stick up for your rights, but also know when to be passive and cooperative. Respect and consider the advice of others, especially your parents.

—*Ann K., 53, Wales, North Dakota*

Love, From Grandma

Enjoy nature and appreciate the beauty it provides. You will only have one lifetime. Fill it full of good memories!

—*Betty B., 78, Sun City, Arizona*

Experience as many new adventures as you can.

—*Karol W., 52, Everett, Washington*

First rule of life: "Don't sweat the small stuff."
Second rule of life: "Everything is small stuff."

—*Charlotte D., 59, Dayton, Ohio*

"Give to the world the best you have
and the best will come back to you."
Practice the following:
1. Honesty
2. Unselfishness
3. Fairness
4. Compassion
5. Integrity
6. Self-discipline
7. Divine belief

—*Margaret F., 80, Melbourne, Florida*

Have fun. Don't take yourself or anyone else too seriously.

—*Sue S., 57, Roseville, Minnesota*

Health and happiness are not guaranteed in this life. You will have to recognize the good things and take time to appreciate them. It's not what you have or how much you have but who you have to share them with.

You have to think for yourself. The leaders of today are not always what they should be in government, religion, and all avenues of life. You must make your own decisions knowing that you will have to live with them.

It seems like many things come back to you again and again; what goes around comes around. Also, what you feel today is not how you will always feel about things. Your understanding of life will change throughout your life.

—Lorelie A., 54, Hastings, Minnesota

Life is a mystery to be lived, not a puzzle to be solved.

—Kaye O., 66, Chicago, Illinois

I believe that life is an exciting adventure. There are valleys and peaks and we must have a zest for life as well as a positive attitude and a love and faith in God. With these things we can always know even in our most trying times that there is always a light at the end of the tunnel. Look for the good in others and, most important, have confidence in yourself. Like your_self_.

—*Karen W., 47, Detroit, Michigan*

I have always tried to set a good example and to give advice through action and not through words. I think it lasts longer and is more effective. "Action speaks louder than words."

—*Tillie T., 80, Newman Grove, Nebraska*

Stay busy. Keep inquiring about life and its good options. Dress neatly.

—*Eline B., 66, St. Paul, Minnesota*

Love, From Grandma

Keep fit. Keep your body healthy because health and strength are a precious gift. Avoid drugs, alcohol, and sex.

Through life spread a bit of sunshine, some joy, laughter, and, oh yes, there will be tears.

Love is the only thing that abides forever and if we withhold love, we damage our own lives and all those we come in contact with.

I found the following clipping in your grandfather's billfold after he passed away. I treasure it and hope you will too.

Forget the hasty unkind word
Forget the quarrel and the cause
Forget the slander you have heard
Forget the whole affair because
Forgetting is the only way.

—Ruth R., 87, Fort Dodge, Iowa

Find balance in your life. Don't put all your eggs in one basket. Work, leisure, worship, learning, all are part of life; to concentrate on one aspect and ignore the rest is a big mistake.

—*Sandy L., 46, Plymouth, Minnesota*

Learn to rejoice over, or with the daily ordinary things or happenings. Stay hope-filled.

—Marie G., 71, Lamberton, Minnesota

LIFE IS AN ADVENTURE AND A JOURNEY. Good things and some not-so-good things will happen to you on your lifetime journey. Remember, it's not what happens to you that counts. It's how you choose to act and think. Remember the "F" words: Fun and Flexibility.

—rubye E., 61, Edina, Minnesota

Life is very fragile. Live each day as if it is your last on this earth.

—Marlys S., 69, Sun City West, Arizona

Life is beautiful at any age; tough, but beautiful. Keep a positive attitude. It will get you over the rough times and you will live longer.

—Gloria W., 68, Franklin Lakes, New Jersey

Life is difficult, but also wonderful. Life is stressful, but with love, patience, self-confidence, and faith you can overcome the traumas, and life will return to you what you have given of yourself to others.

—*Lorraine W., 79, Minneapolis, Minnesota*

Live life to the fullest, but always be aware of what you are getting into. Now that you are an adult, make sure you try to make this world a better place by your actions. Lead an honest life and you'll never have to back track or cover up your wrongs.

—*Carol B., 52, Elk River, Minnesota*

Live life to the fullest. Love God, love and care for yourself, your family and others, in this order. If you truly love God and yourself, everything else will fall in place.

—*Kathy P., 55, New Market, Alabama*

Live life, smell the roses, travel, laugh, and appreciate all that God has given you.

—*Ruth C., 76, Sioux Falls, South Dakota*

Maintain a balance of spiritual, mental, and physical activities in life; each is important. Have fun and laugh!!

—*Marion D-H., 50, Knoxville, Tennessee*

Most importantly, each day take time to appreciate life and have some fun and laughter!!! Find the humor and joy in every day!

—*Carol P., 56, Harrisville, Rhode Island*

Live today so that you have no regrets tomorrow.

Believe in the triumph of good always.

Express gratitude to family, friends, associates, God.

Have courage.

Fear is the thief of health, peace, joy, judgment, and progress.

—*Becky Ann S., 73, West Lafayette, Indiana*

Make use of the abilities God has given you. Every problem has a solution. Enjoy what is beautiful and believe that as you give to the world, so the world will give to you.

I have a saying that I like:

Do more than exist, live.
Do more than read, absorb.
Do more than touch, feel.
Do more than hear, listen.
Do more than look, observe.
Do more than listen, understand.

—Janahan E., 78, Newman Grove, Nebraska

Protect your virginity for marriage. Seek good things and avoid the bad for a happy and fruitful life.

—Mary Jane B., 74, Chicago, Illinois

Strengthen your mind continuously.

—*Roxann M., 54, Mounds View, Minnesota*

Share what you have and you will always be happy.
"Happiness is not having what you want but wanting what you have."

—*Marian M., 69, Roseville, Minnesota*

Now that you are on your own, don't forget the rules from home. Your parents cannot see the things you are doing, but God can. Your parents trust you. Live up to their trust. Life can be exciting and fun; be sure you use it the right way. The most exciting entertainment and person isn't always the best.
There is never a problem too small or too big to call home about.
You can count on us!

—*Arleen K., 70, Thompson, North Dakota*

Our lives are in process every moment, which means change is ever present. Don't be afraid of change. One usually doesn't recognize the really important moments in one's life until it's too late. Enjoy each day. People often pass up the moment looking too far ahead. We only really have right now.

—*Gerry C., 66, Phoenix, Arizona*

Take care of the little things. The big things take care of themselves!

—*Jackie O., 50, Dawson, Minnesota*

Take time to enjoy the journey.

—*Carol B., 53, Eagan, Minnesota*

Patience is the ability to count down before blasting off. Patience is more than just holding back negative emotions of anger, irritation or hostility; it is being calm. Upsetting, irritating circumstances are bound to be a part of your day-to-day life. Forewarned is forearmed, so try to retreat to your calm.

—*Nellie M., 92, Kanawha, Iowa*

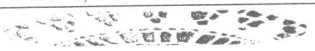

Taking care of yourself is a wonderful way to learn and grow. Have fun, enjoy your accomplishments, and appreciate even the smallest, as well as the greatest accomplishments. Enjoy and appreciate, even celebrate, your mistakes (you will make many, of course), and learn from them. Remember, when you have some tough times and are feeling down and discouraged: 1) that you are loved, and 2) that you can reach out to someone or something for help.

There is always help in many forms available to you.

The things that you do now, both good and bad, will be with you for the rest of your life. Always strive for the balance in your life between God, yourself, good and bad, work and play and remember that your balance is different than anyone else's.

YOU ARE SPECIAL!!!

—Theresa S., 57, Forest Lake, Minnesota

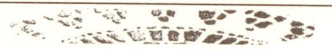

Things and events will sometimes not "go your way," but be a good contestant (a good loser, if necessary) and above all, keep your sense of humor.

—*D. Jane H., 68, Midland, Michigan*

You get out of life what you put into life. Your attitude toward life is in your control. Be positive but also realistic.

—*Mary H., 61, New Ulm, Minnesota*

My father was living proof of his favorite saying: "Don't go anywhere, if you're not going to have a good time. Enjoy life." That held true for him to age 86.

—*Carmen K., 60, Shoreview, Minnesota*

You never have to remember what you've said _if_ you tell the truth. No matter what you have, much or little, share with others. Support charities to the best of your ability.

—*Shirley R., 69, Dayton, Ohio*

Try to have a garden wherever you live. Even if it's a pot on the front step. Plants are good for you and it's good to get your hands dirty now and then. Make sure you have music, too. I don't care what kind it is as long as you like it. Eat right and exercise. Have fun. The kind of fun that makes you feel good. Clean fun, like a really good game of golf. Get a dog. You'll always have someone to come home to that really wants to see you. Find a friend; a real friend you can confide in. You won't need a psychiatrist. (The dog will help too.) When you find that friend, let him or her confide in you. When you look for the love of your life don't look so much at the outside. Look with your heart and when you marry, do so with the idea that you're doing this for life. And when you lose people you love, grieve. Then live and always take joy in the little things God gives you, along with His greater gifts. Care about others. Not just with your money, but with your time. Laugh a lot.

—*Judy R., 47, Breckenridge, Minnesota*

What is a Grandma?

The following was written by a third grader
for a school assignment:

A Grandma is a lady who has no children of her own so she likes other people's little girls. A Grandfather is a man Grandmother. He goes for walks with the boys and they talk about fishing and things like that. Grandma's don't have anything to do except be here. They are so old they should not play hard. It is enough if they drive us to the supermarket where the pretend horse is and have lots of dimes ready or if they take us for walks, they should slow down past pretty things like leaves and caterpillars. They should never say "hurry up." Usually they are fat, but not too fat. They wear glasses and funny underwear. They can take their teeth and gums off. It is better if they don't typewrite or play cards, except with us. They don't have to be smart, only answer questions like why dogs hate cats and how come God isn't married. They don't talk baby-talk like visitors do because it is hard to understand. When they read to us they don't skip words or mind if it is the same story again. Everybody should try to have a Grandma, especially if they don't have a television, because Grandmas are the only grown-ups who have got time.

Thank you to Grandmother Patricia B. of Palmer, Alaska for sending this to us.

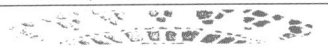

Coming in 1995...
Grandmas: God's Special Angels

Be part of our next book about Grandmothers planned for release in late 1995. It's called *Grandmas: God's Special Angels*. Send us your story about a special memory you have of your grandmother. The story can be about an experience with your grandmother when she was living or when she was no longer with this world.

We are looking for stories about a time or situation you had with your grandmother that was so special you have remembered it as a special or significant time. A time or situation so special, it was as if your grandmother was an angel. It could be a time you spent together that was special, or a time she comforted you, or a place you went together, or a time you felt her spirit with you.

Send your story to: Grandmother Angels
Future Focus Publishing
2626 East 82nd St., #228
Minneapolis, MN 55425-1381

(Be sure to include your address and phone number.)

Or call Becky Amble at Future Focus Publishing:
(612) 858-8877

Ordering Information

To purchase additional copies of *Love, From Grandma* by Becky L. Amble copy or cut this order form, complete it and send to Future Focus Publishing.

The book will be available directly from the publisher, Future Focus Publishing, and may be difficult to find in stores so please, use the order form here. If you like the book, please tell others and feel free to give them a copy of the order form.

Name _____

Address _____

City _____ State _____ Zip _____

In case we have a question, please include your phone number(s):

Daytime phone number (___) _____
Evening phone number (___) _____

(see other side)

Number of books at $10.95 each   _____

Minnesota residents are required to pay
Minnesota sales tax of 6.5%
(.71 for each book)   _____

Shipping and handling
($1.50 for one book,
.75 for each additional book)   _____

Total   _____

Payment method (circle one):

Check   Money order   Credit Card (Visa or MasterCard)

Credit Card Number (16 digits) _____

Expiration date of credit card: _____

Signature of credit card holder _____

Send to: Future Focus Publishing
                 2626 E. 82nd St., #228
                 Minneapolis, MN 55425-1381

Fax orders to (612) 858-8950
Phone orders to (612) 858-8877